Me N'Pieces

Eric Saunders

Stages & Pages Collective

For information regarding permissions, write to:
Stages & Pages Collective LLC
spcollectiveindy@gmail.com

Editor: Nikki Petty-Miles
Cover Designer: Eddie Miles III
Copy Editor: Erica Petty-Saunders and Nikki Jones

Library of Congress Control Number: 202393247
ISBN 979-8-218-17363-0

Dedication

Dedicated to everything that I have been through over the course of my life. To the many people, many inspirations and many situations along the way. To my mother for choosing, protecting and preparing me. For my wife and children, I pray this collection serves as a photo album of pieces of my soul that guide you to me if ever we get lost. For the joy you bring to my burdened heart. To Momma Nikki for accepting me and raising me while pulling back the cloak of poetry for me to see.

To Nazeah, Shaunette and the car ride down to Bloomington, Indiana when you asked "you ready for this?" Eclectic Poetic forever. For my DAY ONES and the love that's unmeasured. To the DAY AFTER DAY ONES who have pushed and supported me. To anyone I've mentored or encouraged to write or at least look at life with depth. To the NAPTOWN poets and Kafe Kuumba. To the elder poets and griots who spoke to my soul and passed along a sip of poetry.

To my matriarchs Mae Freeman and Marie Saunders who placed the fishing pole in my hand. To Daniel Saunders Jr., for a foundation of character. To Victor Glover, for being what Darth Vader was to Luke Skywalker.

As you've done since the beginning...

KEEP SHINING FULL POWER SUPREME!

Foreword

I am thrilled to introduce my dear friend and talented poet, Eric Saunders, and his awe-inspiring poetry collection. Eric and I go way back to our days at Indiana University Bloomington. I was first struck by his boundless creativity and ability to use language to evoke emotion and meaning.

As members of the poetry group Eclectic Poetic, we worked together for years on the Indiana poetry scene, fusing music with spoken word and contributing to the culture of performance art. Eric's work consistently left us in awe with its depth, complexity, and insightful musings. His ability to craft poetic masterpieces that resonate with people of all ages is truly a gift, and I have no doubt that this latest publication will be no exception.

Eric's multifaceted nature is evident not only in his writing but also in his visual art and in every aspect of his life. His unwavering commitment to activism, justice, and equality is admirable. I am honored to have traveled alongside him to different universities and colleges, fighting for the causes that are close to our hearts.

As you delve into the pages of this poetry collection, be prepared to be transported to other worlds, as Eric's words have the power to transcend time and place. Every line, every word, and every image is carefully crafted to elicit the most profound emotions, inspiring readers to reflect on the world around them and to take action toward making it a better place.

Eric's poetry collection is an extraordinary achievement, a testament to his exceptional writing skills, and his ability to weave powerful narratives into his work. I highly recommend this collection to poetry and spoken word enthusiasts worldwide!

Eric, my friend, congratulations on this well-deserved accomplishment. You are an inspiration to all of us, and I eagerly anticipate your future works.

Sincerely,

Naz Khalid

The Moving Finger writes; and having writ, Moves on: nor all thy Piety nor Wit Shall lure it back to cancel half a Line, Nor all thy Tears wash out a Word of it. – Omar Khayyam

Delay

So sorry for the delay, got caught up
trying to make sense of all the bumps and the falls
of the past while walking in the present.

The tears and tissues, parental abandonment issues,
didn't know neglect, or abuse, just be
better days that felt like hog head cheese on crackers
while fishing with elders or,
vegetable soup to heal the croup cough.

My grandmother made sure I was fed,
to add to that, she ensured I was nourished with
respect in my head when greeting others, sharing with my brothers.
No abuse, sometimes confused with the words adults used
so occasionally called mf's, sissy, and fool, still grew strong
and observed the multiple tools used to teach me right from wrong.

I rode bikes, flew kites and sang songs to make decisions,
in essence, the bubble gum, bubble gum
in a dish may have kept me out of prison,
certainly, a catalyst for developing vision,
focus less on the bubble gum, should've done more wishing
then, so that now, life would not feel like a delay.

I taught myself how to pray
by repeating the Our Father on the bathroom wall at home
and, later on, began to meditate in the 11th grade
not bad when you were raised to go to church the holy way
for just Easter and Christmas holidays.

Got delayed at the side of my mother's death bed,
with staples across her head trying to survive,
I was like 10 then feeling like 25,

praying that God would keep my mother alive
and He did.

Delayed when seeing my father handcuffed and dressed up in orange
in court sentenced to serve a bid
with a face of desperation,
I prayed for his restoration
and sometime later found myself outside the prison gates
waiting to take him back home.

Delayed when he was forced by bullets to touch heaven's gates
to meet his mother back home.

And I guess my mind has been on delay
in spite of the fact that God has shown up on multiple occasions,
in multiple ways and situations
progress was still being made.

Some say,
I should've been writing this way,
way before today,
I can respond with, well my great grandmother
Mae did use to say,
"The Lawd works in mysterious ways."
In retrospect, I'm more blessed in a major way,
and full of reasons to celebrate with praise.

I learned to drive through the traffic of yesterday
I'm here now.

Sorry for the delay.

Poets

Poets don't just talk to you,
but speak to the light in your eyes, so
that it reflects the light from our eyes,
onto your heart.

Dreams to Hope
(Young adult self-talk)

When I grow up,
I want to surpass the stars,
look down one time to see,
how far we've come.

A dream was for my cuz
to go to the league,
a hope for my cuz,
was to never bleed.

To succeed, what does it mean?
Where is that place?
When I was younger,
it was written all over my face.

From value, to dreams, hopes and virtues,
momma always said, somebody will try to hurt you.
I'm grown up now.
What should I do?

I don't have a plan.
How must I stand?
When I go home,
I must be the man.

But I'm scared.

WAIT!!!
Wait one minute,
don't quit there son,
cause you're still in it,
you look left and then right,

but you must look above
yeah, people like you, but you
only need God's love.

So don't be like the rest,
you must beat all the rest,
open yo' mind and look in your chest,
every hope you have,
don't stir them aside
don't be scared, don't fret
boy please don't hide.

Keep your dreams,
for only they keep you alive.

Sincerely,

Pride

Dark Child
1994

MAY, Mother's Day, my mother laid on a hospital bed,
tubes injected all through her arms
staples zipped in forehead.

With a 10 year-old mind,
first time aneurysm crossed mine,
let alone finding out it can kill you from within.

My mother did not die then.
She became the 1% that survive when,
99% have a ship of death to fly in.

Imagine, the world and the size when,
this all collides, in a fifth grader's mind, when stressed
of making at least B's in math and science.

I do believe that was the day,
my heart was hardened to loner ways,
just a year before I was moved away,
in survival mode UP my mind was made
even then in affirmation,
now motivated me to see life with more foresight
young integrity to ignore wrong and to do more right.

Ignite passion prosper with sheer will and bravery,
shackles broken, mind elevated to be
more than slavery,
so it amazes me.

LOOK AT ME
Look through me,
and don't stare lazily,
don't prepare questions to ask
look beyond THESE masks.

Do you even see a DARK CHILD?

A weed wild with crooked foundation,
and listens with fear,
fear of the unknown and its borders,
fear of responsibility,
fear to fail to be responsible,
considering it was me and baby bro
at the hospital,
got a little dark that day
became comforted by silence cold and mellow
(Melancholy taste like Americano)
a teddy bear and tears on my pillow,
a bit of woe is me was seeded
now having such pride in such a pain,
is such a destructive way to be conceited,
started off small with my age
realized overtime, time begins to feed IT.

Dark Child never faded,
but subconsciously feasted,
attached to my back
using my organs to eat with and legs to walk on,
speaks directly to my desires before needing a tongue to talk on,

hard to walk on clouds
when backs grow rooted into the ground,
trees can only go so far up.

I've worked so hard to work so far away from my full potential,
to stepping back and forth, forth and back
this Dark child, on my back, looks down
deeper into ground found in foundations of
Greed
Lust
Pride
Avarice
Vanity
Wrath
all eat with Gluttony's intent,
comfortable working with nothing,
knowing that Mr. Saunders needs to be something.

I was 28 when I first started writing this poem and now...
40 re-intertwine into now,
a husband now,
a father now.

I'm embracing a gift that needs cultivation,
and up until this day,
I've mastered my day to day,
wiggling within the ways of righteousness, and the wages of sin
got a force within that gets dizzy from running from the forces of self-
made enemies that have kept me down,
who I know systematically will shut down,
drown and bow down the instant Mr. Saunders rises from the ground,

GOD given and poetically dripping,
declaration that I'm coming to get my divine crown,
not just these remolded teeth,
but this darkness deep
beneath this Dark Child
growing strong,
but with gentle recklessness.

Through the process
of becoming weak each and every week,
reek of each pornographic peek,
each drive and drink,
bask in the ambiance of weed for grief,
each moment to cheat
12 o'clock ice cream and meat,
leads to clogged arteries.

Jealousy for those that actually
live life then take pride in these lies,
rocking back-and-forth,
angry as if this is the day I die,
or submit to suicide.

Dark Child been building its growth
since that day in 1994 of hurt and hope
lodged in the hurt stuck in curiosity of mediocrity
to soothe it,
affective abuse in this repetitive music,
prolonged position in time
ready the corner man's towel,
to be tossed in to lose it,

dragging me to the brink of death
reaching for the tip of my last breath.

This all nestles itself

in the webs of my minds complex,

but then I realize that it is because of the 1%

left that hope still can progress.

Firmly I believe, I'm still here because of God's grace and mercy
be strong now in the midst of self-infliction,
this gift has been waiting,
Dark Child be buying tickets to be wicked,
sitting, and time is only ticking,
before fully embracing God's permission
to take steps across dimensions
stronger than ever I imagine
with a Dark Child's division,
just time to fly high, do something different.

We see too many loved ones
come within inches of setting their souls to a death, long slave
sentence,
so I set forth free as my intention,
particular methods to ravel in vengeance,
mouth open, fist clenching, heart loving, ears listen,
mind soul connected to intergalactic perception,
immortal motivation to strike the injustice of insurrections.

I'm not giving up
I'm my mothers child, I can't quit
I'm my fathers wit,

with faith the size of a mustard seed.

I say DARK CHILD,
you've lived your dreams with venomous ambition,
option A is to concede , but since I know you won't listen,
no weapon formed against me shall prosper, you got to go quick like
cheddar biscuits in the first 5 minutes at Red Lobster,
I can't masquerade with you no more around town,
yep, I'm still my brothers keeper
but it's about to get gangsta now,
lay down or get down.

The 1% of life I've seen now controls the 99% adversary of
self-destruction, without you I can function,
and this decree has been read off.

Don't call CPS or 911,
just turn away, if you're too afraid
to witness me cut this
Dark Child's head clean OFF!

No Happy Poems

Well, if you came for happy poems,
I ain't got no happy poems.

All I got is these bologna sammiches
of a life I was born to find joy in.
In spite of all the worrying before praying.

All I got is all the extra stuff that I just smashed between
these two last pieces of bread,
some will call it the crusty part bread or the booty bread but....
considering that the beginning has officially met the end
I call them,
the ALPHA and OMEGA bread.

And it's only right, that in between all this stuff
on this sammich, and falling off the sides
is still held together by Christ.
Giving new meaning to the bread of life.

I just be walking through these windows
further away from hurt
I found the moments
I got knocked down
with rocks and words,
lies and tears,
trauma after trauma, and the rise of fears,
still found my smile in the middle of recess,
found in moments of stress, and big stress.

Found in history of broken dreams and broken necks,
just for me to wake up with freedom laying in my bed,
you'll find me winning with no permission, and no wishes
just floating through dark dimensions,

trying to find my way to my wife's kisses.

You'll find moments where I should've been dead,
but only found grace and mercy instead,
the places where foolishness led,
and I can't even begin to list the crazy things in my head,
and the crazy things I did.

Found forgiveness and patience
And a WHOLE LOT,
I MEAN A WHOLE LOT OF PEOPLE HATING
just because I was born
you'll only find I've been torn,
hurt but never tortured,
hurt knowing that others have been tortured.

You'll find me numb and in pieces,
just as you'll find me sweeping and gluing back my pieces,
you'll find my smile with my kids,
nephews and nieces,
students and mentees,
you'll find I had to learn my own path.
Seven sins deep from gluttony to envy
to wrath.

You'll find yourself feeling like me
when you think about all you've been through,
just to relocate a laugh.
You'll find fools talking to you like a fool
so much that you'll think
you are one, until you actually begin to fly
learn to run, learn to escape,
and call it fun.

In spite of the hate that someone dumb enough tried to take

and mistake you for a lost cause,
insignificant and irrelevant,
you'll find a taste of that same bologna sammich in your face.

This is a story of taste, and I'm telling it.

Keep on living as the elders say,
as they taught me how to cast
at 5 a.m. when the world is quiet and the fish are biting.
But how to be calm when the rain comes,
and how to reel it back when it seems to be getting away from you,
reminds you of moments that life had you shook,
but let that fish nibble and take that bait
down and let it hook itself.

Oh no, I got no happy poems,
just how we made it over poems,
just how we found our grit poems,
how you found yourself poems,
how we can't just say happy birthday,
but do what you was supposed to do,
and KEEP SHINING FULL POWER SUPREME POEMS.

How you shine be it spark or flame or star,
when life was dark and hard, and harden hearts
concrete constantly, consistently.

And yet this sammich taste like
JOY AND PAIN.
LIKE SUNSHINE AND RAIN.
SAY IT TO ME,
SAY IT TO ME,
JOY AND PAIN,
LIKE SUNSHINE AND RAIN,
poems.

Snowy Road
December 1999

The love of others warms me as I go,
grateful I am, but I must beat the snow,
but life to this, How does it relate?

I must leave now because it controls my fate.

I pray.

My journey of life begins on a snowy road,
I see that this is a road that others also chose to fight
to go reach my destination, endlessly with little hesitation,
now, like life there are bumps and rocks
I must go around, I am caught in a ditch,
but I pull myself out of the ground.

The devil is at my feet trying to lead me astray,
God is all over me, and I am back on my way,
to reach home is my end and my fate is sealed,
from a snowy road, my life is revealed.

About the Way I Feel
1999

Do you know?
Naw!
You wouldn't,
and if you even tried your best to know you couldn't.

People are just stressing along with me,
passing judgment on what you don't see.

Unrighteous to fight this feeling deep inside,
I feel scared, so I'm going to hide.

But I say,
Who am I?
I know.
I feel.

Strengthen my spirit and keep it real!
So real,
so real,
like the hardest steel!

Just a little, about the way
I feel.

If I'm Being Honest

Truth is,
I've not learned to heal, just keep going on
by and by.

Truth is,
hurt feels more like a scab that fades into skin
and becomes a mark of pain over time,
I meditate mostly, stretch and practice yoga
because my soul holds a desire to be whole,
and balance is key, flexibility compliments longevity.

Truth is,
I'm at war with everything,
and triggering residue is everywhere.

Truth is,
I've been lonely, lost in the dark, in love
and in my thoughts,
I've harbored more pain than I can dock,
constant state of shock,
looks like watching blood run down walls
until it runs dry.

Truth is,
I'm numb with no warning signs
often a tingling in my toes
and solar plexus.

Truth is,
masking hurt more when
everyone thinks you're "perfectly fine",
and "I'm just okay" and "perfectly fine",
ALLLLLL the time!

Truth is,
Fragility has no form,
and I'm not well just because I'm present and because
I got PTO and,
it was a month ago that my brother felt the only choice
was to go by his own hands.

Truth is,
I want to throw it all away,
and stop lying as to why
my face is dry, but I haven't
stopped crying right here in plain sight.

Held Up

Hold up, all the tension
of love's dimension,
not to mention
being held up by the creation
of love's intimidation,
my ultimate legislation,
is my waiting intimidation,
which drives me to bust
from this fornication.

Love's Let Down

Breathe,
take ya time or just leave,
got me trippin' on what love led me to believe,
I grieve and emotionally bleed
for love I can never achieve.
damn sometimes I can't
breathe.

So, then I try to leave it alone,
let it be gone, then play it cool,
but my grief always holds its own.

My shine is then never shown,
chillin to the pain of grief listening to
another love song
I want to love, but love
has played the game to mislead.

I want, I want, want many
things to supply as greed and to
my love's let down,
what you want, is
not always what you…
I need love.

I Know

Boy don't ya know you got dem pretty eyes?

I know.

Boy don't ya know dat you just fine?

Yeah, I know.

Boy don't ya know dat you blessed?!

Thank you, Jesus!!
I know!!

And He ain't done yet.

Don't I know!

With

With me....

I feel a new level of confidence within myself,
this is a crossroads station in my life.

I feel happy now in spite of grief,
I feel a heavy load lifted off my back
all while carrying the world on my shoulders.

With my family...

I really anticipated seeing my family,
again to see how I will wear off on them,
and I feel that I will be able to communicate with them though I will
deeply miss my family here.

With God...

I feel I can trust the Lord,
more so now more than ever,
He knew these days would come,
now I know, and I feel we will be deeper.

Poem

My soul and melody
just be connected sometimes,
and they dance dance dance
until the universe shakes...

How impressive is that?
But I dance anyway,
and to me,
that must be one hell of a beautiful song.

Strange But So
2000

Life to me means a whole other perspective,
though to many lives are hard, crazy and hectic.

The life we live, what are we taught, do you believe?
Morals, what do they mean, what must we achieve?

God's unchanging hand
may set your worries free,
though many may fight for what ain't right.

To end life young or old, to rest in peace hot or cold,
to live a life weak or bold,
and dance on that thin line in the middle, dancing invigorates
me.

That in between is strange but so.
Strange but so.

Reflect me
2000

I am learning now, I start to grow,
not my arms, legs, hands, and feet.

I feel the change inside me, not rare, but slow,
winning is a part of defeat, but here I go.

"Cut your hair nigga," they say.

It Reflects Me!!
Something I can't explain,
it is a part of me, and it's mine,
shows I have a lot on my mind.

I am growing, gonna let my light shine,
and when you see me, what do you see physically?

Don't fool yourself, look through me,
impossible, it's made of brick and not glass,
brick by brick, built knowledge by the past
and elders' laughter heard throughout eternity.

I understand now, that reflects me.

At last.

I Don't Know

By the life I live by....
it becomes so confusing,
how people run past me laughing...
and make me laugh,
kind of amusing,
it tries to defuse me,
defuse my life through the diffusement of my soul.

But,
when I check,
I'm still in progress because,
it's that things change, and
wonder if the change involves me,
in life you are faced with the decision,
or choice to change.

Who will I, or
you be when the time comes
to make the decision,
to decide if my decision
is not based on the choice of change that decided
that it is not your, my decision to choose?!

But to decide.

Downward

Don't lose control of what you have.

Times that provide the best of roughness, seize the moment with all your toughness and stand tall.

Pressure.... of life and the challenge to oneself that it provides.
I want to believe I want to achieve all that I can,
but the pressure weighs me down.

Down until I can no longer stand on my own,
I look to God and ask for forgiveness and strength,
strength to outlast the road of length.

The devil is wise, but does not understand,
I am only moved by God's unchanging hand.

The pressure to succeed increases with pressure to fail,
it becomes a greed to prevail.

But I will.

I have once again gained control,
control of my fate,
all things are able through God,
so it can't stop me.

My journey continues.

Dive

I'm about to dive deep
into foreign places,
located all around substance of the seen and unseen
within me.

Within God's will
that I have not been able to afford to go
before today.

Now!
Right now!
Maybe later.

That's what hesitation whispers,
echoing the same exchange as fear and timidity,
so often reaps mediocrity.

I'm at a standstill,
a middle ground,
in this valley
within mountains,
higher above the ground
where I started from,
and I'm aiming for.

The place where my soul was born,
my destiny, and
I probably can see it clearer
from the top of the mountain.
Because now,
I'm growing wiser.
STANDING HERE

where it hurts to learn of balance
of growing pains.

And I imagine if I keep standing here
then I will forfeit my dive,
deep into a place
where I find something
similar to my reflection.

Maybe with a little more hope,
faith, courage and little discipline.

Developed foresight,
reversed insight,
inscribed in love,
and joy
and peace.

And I'm sure if I dive deep,
I'll find myself somewhere on the other side of the universe,
just a little brighter,
just how I imagine myself.

To be now,
maybe
right now.

Sacrifice

I'm the coon man,
the darkie working in the afternoon man,
the thing you saw in the dark moving,
under that white milk moon man,
If something don't change soon man,
and I MEAN SOON MAN....
I might just go BOOM MAN, BOOM MAN!
Now hand me that hoe next to yo toe man.

I Am

To you, the color of this page.

The slave you enslaved,
from their birth to their grave,
wherever that may be or whatever you care not to see,
which is me, with a damn identity.

What's that mean to you?
Hell, we'll be dead soon with,
his 9 braids, baggy pants, N$ke shoes,and gold tooth.

I see it's been twisted
you must have been misled,
what is shown is never known.

You love Jesse, oh well he can hold his own,
but that goes on everyday, if you are quiet, ok, cool
it will just go away.

Well in 18 days you'll try to label me a statistic,
real funny to put black paint on
your white face as a gimmick of the
Black race you mimic.

Took to the past bring it back again
to when you knew about Malik-Shabazz,
last grin, did nothing because he
was aware of your sin.

Never will I rest,
do my best, though
true, don't ever call me your slave,
acknowledge that I will be Black and not behave.

History never lies, thanks for my pretty eyes.

Uncle LeRoy
Memoirs from 2008...

I came down here to San Antonio, Texas to clear my mind and enjoy some quiet time. I like coming to Texas, it's a recharge for me, but the question is what will happen when I'm charged up. It's like running in circles really fast sometimes. Hamster wheel like. If you're not careful, stress from home will follow you to your vacation spot if you let it.

Just so happens, my Uncle Leroy is in town too. He is my grandfather's much older brother; they have different fathers. I spoke to Uncle Leroy for about an hour straight or so over a couple glasses of Chivas Regal. It's the only hard liquor he drinks. He says it's smooth. He is 83 years old, in good shape and his mind is still pretty sharp. He has such a feeble frame and tries to stay out of the way to observe everything in front of him. He wears glasses that still show his eyes that turned blue from the wisdom (or cholesterol) over time.

His skin is a dark chocolate, and his black is rich with depth. He has surely lived. We had a real conversation, and I was not expecting him to be here in San Antonio. We talked about life, standards, and women. We'd never strongly connected because he's been living in California for about 40-50 years. Turns out he is a World War II veteran. He wishes the draft would come back because too many brothers lack discipline. Makes sense I guess; I'd rather see more brothers in armed service uniforms than penitentiary uniforms.

He spoke of Dorsey Miller, World Word II veteran who was a cook in Pearl Harbor. Yeah, he was a black man and he got killed too.

Uncle Leroy said he had just lost his lady friend to cancer back in February. They would have dinner in his apartment every night. Since then, he has not eaten much, and what he does eat is really processed. I can tell he is lonely because he loves to talk to anyone that will listen. We have never actually talked, so I listen and learn on the back patio in the late afternoon.

A warm afternoon with gentle cool breeze comforts our conversation. We sat near the grill, and even had some Heineken with our Chivas Regal, waiting for the turkey to finish being smoked. This turned out to be our first and only conversation, and instead of just sitting on the wall the flies just danced on and around us the entire time.

Almost Too Real
2000

Man, I'm tired of how things are.
Weakened by stress I can't go that far.
My car needs gas, my pockets need money.
I'm tired, I'm crying, but this ain't funny!
I'm broke when I get paid.
I'm hot when I'm in shade.
I'm lost when I've been found.
Up when I'm on the ground.
I'm cool but I'm really wet.
I saw it but haven't seen it yet.
I'm here but I'm really gone.
In your face but never shown.
By myself and not my own.
Just a child who is getting grown.
I felt but didn't feel.
Just almost too real.

What Love?

We be created
in the image of
the mighty GOD.
So, we must be love,
because God is love.
And so,
we are love.
We all be in the light as love.
So, can I make love to you?
Absolutely not,
because how can we make
what we already are?

Orbit

I can see stars shine tomorrow,
and in 20, 30 or more years from now
when her eyes wear her soul like stems
that hold up flowers.

I'm hopeful,
that life is certainly worth living,
worth feeling like I can,
grab a piece of heaven,
before my heart stops forever
just by holding her hand.

I caught her threading her love
to the fabric of my heart,
yet, and still far from the core
of my heartbeats, but
I believe her persistence shall prevail.

She treats my soul like the
Earth's orbiting moon,
what seemed so impossible
becomes completed soon.

Let it Be
For Daniel Saunders Jr
(Daddy)

12/12/13 Attended doctor's appointment. She spoke to him directly like he comprehends. Discovered one medicine was not there. Took away one ibuprofen 200mg, and aspirin 325mg. Went to McDonald's.

12/16/13 Brought two sausage biscuit sandwiches.

12/17/13 Cut his hair, and he told me the cable was back on. Dirty pants and belt, but alert to the Pacer's loss. Reluctant to let me help sort his medicine. Medicine box in braille, we need a new one. Two different blood pressure pills. Some lady gave him a different one. No Mirtazapine in the pill bottle. One Hydrocodone pill left.

12/18/13 Sold truck for $400 to Big Red Towing. Has a receipt for it. $250, and $150 after title.

12/23/13 Went to the store to pay phone bill. Shopped and bought pancake syrup and water. Debit card would not work. Did not believe me, but then it registered to him. Tried to get gift cards at McDonalds. Talked to my aunt, his sister, she suggested a Power of Attorney. He called later insisting I take him to McDonald's.

1/3/14 Took him to the bank, grocery store, McDonald's and back home.

1/4/14 Picked him up with my wife and child. Went to the dollar store, gas station, McDonald's, my grandmother's house, and then back home.

1/9/14 Days after the ice storm. Had food to eat but took him to McDonald's to get food. He won some money. He knows that he won some money. He wanted to go to the dollar store, and I said no. He told me that he missed his meeting for his recertification at his apartment. I read the letter. His rent could possibly be raised. I have to strongly consider assisted living. I was aggravated because I want to go home, but he would not get out of the car, and the housing situation. It was like it is just one more thing. It was just frustrating. Looked up assisted living homes.

1/31/14 Took him to McDonald's. Got food set-up through CICOA.

2/26/14 Took daddy to the doctor. It was discussed that his level is at a 9, which indicates that he should not be living alone. The family should seek strict supervision options. I took him to McDonald's and home. He asked me to go to church on this Sunday, and I tried to respectfully decline, but he wasn't trying to hear it. He kept trying to form a response for my question of why he wanted me to go. He kept saying "some guy" and "you know and food". I saw him look off and his hand tremble. I could only guess what he was going to say because he never got around to actually saying it. But he finished with a sharp look to me and said "ok!".

I've grown bold now, but more like a new lion primed enough to know the old lion is no longer fit for battle. No longer able to regard his life as if he is locked in a one-dimensional perspective of death. It will come as it comes of course, but how far death goes to lurk around the corners to those dealing with dementia.

Even though no one wants to watch a wounded animal suffer, it can be troublesome to lean on that perspective alone. Now all we have to do is be there to make him as comfortable as possible because that's healthy and compassionate. He deserves this. If my daddy does not have dementia, then maybe something can still be done about his affinity to McDonald's sausage biscuit, pancakes (with butter and strawberry jelly), and 2 hamburgers with grape jelly.

When the Rain Comes

When the rain comes,
I'd wish you not to think of the worst,
just because the sun ain't out (too hot anyway).

Let rest and oh Lord let it rain,
but when it comes,
some want to love,
but others hate it
because it ruined their plans.

But what you don't understand
is the power present when the rain comes,
damn, it snows, I miss the rain.

I feel the tease that January brings,
and I need the rain simply because,
my struggles, my pains, temptations,
and sins have covered
my body with presence,
covers my light and any essence.

So dry me sun,
cause the rain is coming in,
wash me rain,
please help me
feel clean again.

Cope

Too many sweets and TV,
especially after nine.

Smoking consecutive days to cope
too much pain to process
in my mind,
I'd rather hold it tight inside
versus,
placing as much as possible
in between these lines.

I've enjoyed doing nothing
for far too long,
mediocre standard
is a hold too strong.

Strange pleasure
in no moderation
of watching
two rights turn
into a
wrong.

I Am a Loser
To my professional brothers and sisters

Because I am different,
because I choose to be different,
and try to make a difference
in a world where most people
are no different
sit and signify
ridicule the differences of others,
I AM A LOSER.

People talk down to losers, use losers,
and abuse losers, simply hate losers,
losers are different.

Deep down, many people want to be losers,
jealous because of their incapability
to allow themselves to be different
or sacrifice their image.

I'm not trying to be nice
if I am I am.

I don't want to please everybody,
but rather just be a loser in peace,
but folks hate me because I'm truly unique,
I say what I do, and I do what I speak
not a path for the complete.

I do things differently,
still to my own self I be true because,
if being fake and shrewd
is what I have to do to win,
then I just would rather lose.

It does not matter what I do
speak, live or pray,
jealousy of the nearest hater
seems to find a way, to remind me
I AM A LOSER.

I'm a loser, I'm different
yet I'm still the same,
we breathe the same way,
but when you breathe, you speak
you say you love me, then hate me
in the same day.

Like Jason did Freddy,
you can try to stab me in the back,
the same way because,
I AM A LOSER.

My Sun Never Sets

To the observers

Those cats have come and those same cats have failed. They
come up the same path and leave on the same trail.
Well, on my day, prayed over and for the day after! How they
consume my mouth with laughter.

You see, my soul runs deep,
elements of the black sea, strong like the Zambezi your
efforts displease me.

My eyes blaze lit with flame.
Similar to stars that guide to freedom's hand.
OMMMM to my 3rd eye to understand,
my hair is rougher than Sahara sand,
where once a boy stood now stands a man,
like a Tuesday evening's darkness,
without effort I haunt your mind,
thoughts of enslaving you makes you step behind!
I transcend into a mind that dare not run,
but walk, pace and take my time.
Through time I remain broken in body,
but spirit still intact.
Insist in your attack to sit attached to my back
I'm trapped in your night, but I'm not done yet.

Though your moon may rise.
My sun never sets.

Jealous of Them
To my Dad

As I began to walk the halls,
cruise the malls,
I hear cries from a child who falls,
Then crying stands still when he lands in…
…a man's hands,
his father's hands.

In my mind I try to find a
close tide to bind, search again,
until the thought bends of a
father and friend.

If I fall like a child, the pain I would
hate it, in that moment, just trade it, for a
father and the son he created.

I fell and I could only cry,
I can't breathe, can't believe, can't stand,
can't see my father's hands.

Son to Mother
To Mom, Thanks Langston ...1998

I'm sorry mother,
you see I never realized that
you endure those rainy days,
to provide me with better skies.

My father is gone,
that leaves you,
hard enough to be a mother, but that parent too.

Mother, how do you do it?
Those steps were bare,
worked hard for me, my sister and brothers,
even for others, you didn't care.

I was ashamed in front of others, I felt poor, broke and black.
Grateful I am for my shoes, food and my coat on my back.

Soak in hope, to provide better days, in ways not understood,
my ways are praised by your blessings, your maze.
I'm amazed and it's all good.

So now you stand tall, dirty steps and all,
many times fall, only to rise and stand, claim land for
your son, a man, and a new generation.

Thank you mother with all my appreciation.

Makings of Me.... Affirmations from Others
High School Senior Retreat 2001

Eric you are

Unique, skilled, a renaissance man
Fabulous, an author, and phenomenal,
Wonderful, admirable, a shepherd,
Inspirational, beautiful, a leader,
Embodied spirit, future filled, and comforting
A difference-maker, classic and sophisticated,
Amazing, concerned, and goal-oriented
Strong, magnificent, and athletic
Inspiring, capable and talented
Trustworthy, poetic and special
Well-expressed, friendly, and articulate
Deep, dominate and limitless
Artistic, genuine and awesome
Real, likable and humorous
Helpful, outspoken, and funny
Caring, Unexpected, and Influential
Advanced, talented and you make others feel good about themselves. Honest,
prayed for and mature
People person, faith-filled and grace-filled
An Inspiration, good example and generous
You represent originality, ingenuity and wisdom
You are "Jesus Christ Christmas Stocking" advice-filled and deep full of faith and
determination.
Remove obstacles Upfront LIVE THE FOURTH!
"Blessed be the Lord, who daily loads us with benefits" Psalms 68:19 (Like you Eric)

To the Lord

To my creator and through God the maker of all things, I am able to rejoice. You have blessed me with the skill of expression through dance, song, and writing.

I am fortunate to have a friend and Father in you. The older I get, the wiser I become. As I become wiser, I begin to know a little more about myself, about you.

Thank you for the obstacles that will be present in my life, and Lord please place your unchanging hand on me so that we can get over them.

Amen

Leaving you with this thought...

For over 20 years, poetry and I have been on and off. Not sure what I was looking for, but once I would write a poem, it appeared that it was looking for me. Taking pieces of my mind, heart and soul and leaving them to the world as evidence that I was here. Like the greats before such as Langston Hughes, Amiri Baraka and Mari Evans, I noticed how one's consciousness lives through the words. I noticed how those very powerful words can change the trajectory of the reader and paint endless moments in time.

These pieces of poetry are pieces of me as I've walked along this journey searching for myself. At this moment, I walk with a hole in my spirit as a result of losing my father to homicide. Each day I'm seeking every inch of joy in an effort to be whole. Poetry has been a gift. It's brought more opportunities than I can remember, but more importantly it has connected me to other lovers of poetry and art. It's allowed me to see itself in the substance of life. Anchoring itself to my heart in times of grief, joy, confusion and anger. Showing me how to feel, that I can feel, and I can even heal. Heal from, through and in darkness while being guided in the spark of light in my heart.

I currently stand in a place where I can aim forward and upward with poetry. Much can be achieved, and this gift ultimately passes through me and into the heart of the next reader. Prayerfully landing in the heart of the poets that come after me. The future may study me, I don't know. Here is where it begins, and where my consciousness lives beyond my life.